FINCHLEY & FRIERN BARNET

A Pictorial History

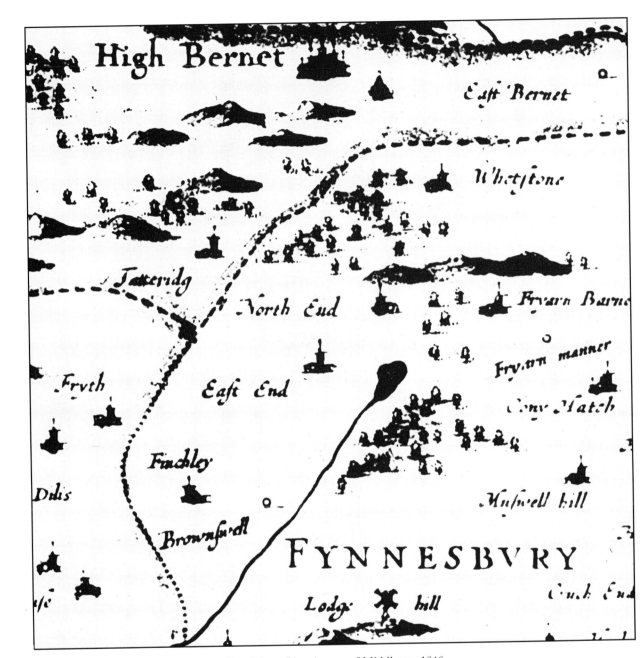

Detail from Blaeu's map of Middlesex, 1646.

FINCHLEY
&
FRIERN BARNET
A Pictorial History

Stewart Gillies and Pamela Taylor

Barnet Libraries Arts and Museums

Phillimore

1992

Published by
PHILLIMORE & CO. LTD.
Shopwyke Hall, Chichester, Sussex

ISBN 0 85033 844 1

Printed and bound in Great Britain by
BIDDLES LTD.
Guildford, Surrey

To all those, past, present and future,
who share our enthusiasm for the history of this area.

List of Illustrations

Frontispiece: Detail from Blaeu's map of Middlesex, 1646

1. John Rocque's map of 1754
2. Dollis Brook, *c.*1905
3. The ford, Dollis Brook, 1904
4. Beating the Friern Barnet bounds, 1910
5. Beating the Finchley bounds, 1934-5
6. St James' church, Friern Barnet, 1779
7. St James' church, Friern Barnet, 1892
8. St Mary at Finchley church, exterior, *c.*1880
9. St Mary at Finchley, interior, *c.*1900
10. Finchley Manor House, *c.*1900
11. The Avenue, *c.*1904
12. Friern House, 1797
13. Cherry Tree Wood, *c.*1926
14. Railway Cottages, 1905
15. High Road East Finchley at The Bishop's Avenue, *c.*1910
16. Sketch of the encampment on Finchley Common, 1780
17. Dispersion of Dissenters' meeting on Finchley Common
18. Turpin's Oak, early 19th century
19. Turpin's Oak, 1873
20. A deed of 1498
21. The Finchley almshouses, 1895
22. The Campe almshouses
23. A cottage near Finchley, 1779
24. King John's House, 1903
25. The *Green Man*, early 20th century
26. The burglary at Mr. Clewin's, 1778
27. Oak Lodge, 1947
28. The Grange, *c.*1905
29a. Fallow Lodge, *c.*1870
29b. The Goodyear family at Fallow Lodge, *c.*1870
30. Fallow Farm, *c.*1900
31. Russell Lane, early 20th century
32. Squires Lane, *c.*1907
33. Swan Lane in the 1930s
34. Coppetts Farm
35. The Woodhouse, 1797
36. Plasterwork at Woodhouse
37. Coldharbour, 1938
38. Whetstone, *c.*1880
39. Timber framing at 1264 High Road Whetstone, 1989
40. Whetstone tollhouse, 1863
41. Hendon Lane and Regents Park Road, *c.*1911
42. The *Torrington Arms*, mid-19th century
43. The *Torrington Arms*, early 20th century
44. The *White Lion*, 1825
45. The *Bald Faced Stag*, 1878
46. Market Place looking north
47. Market Place looking south
48. The Walks, early 20th century
49. Elmhurst, 1939
50. Park House
51. Selina Villa, mid-19th century
52a. Falkland House, 1894
52b. The Tate family at Falkland House, 1894
53. Grove House
54. Moss Hall sale catalogue, 1824
55. Brent Lodge
56. Colney Hatch Asylum, mid-19th century
57. The laundry room at Colney Hatch Asylum
58. The Avenue, 1965
59. The lake at Woodside, mid-19th century
60. St John's church, Whetstone, 1930
61. Torrington Cottage, 1949
62. Cottages on High Road North Finchley, 1886
63. North Finchley Congregational church diaconate, *c.*1914
64. Dale Grove Hall, *c.*1870
65. Christ Church, *c.*1870
66. Park Place, 1818
67. Prospect Place, early 20th century
68. Strawberry Vale, mid-19th century
69. Consecration of St Marylebone cemetery, 1855
70. High Road East Finchley at Church Lane, *c.*1890
71. Traders at Woodbine Cottages, *c.*1910
72a. Holy Trinity church
72b. Holy Trinity school manual, 1851
73. Finchley Hall in the early 20th century
74. Church End, pre-1885
75. St Mary's school
76. Station Road, *c.*1910
77. Crooked Usage, *c.*1913
78. Finchley Bridge, pre-1897
79. Nether Street, *c.*1905
80. The *Orange Tree*, *c.*1903
81. Vine Cottages, *c.*1903
82. St James' school, *c.*1905
83. A class at St James' school in the 1920s

84. Glenroy, 1892
85. Hendon Lane
86. Finchley Garden Village
87. Field Cottage sale catalogue of 1902
88. The Broadway, c.1880
89. The Broadway, c.1908
90. The Broadway, pre-1909
91. The *Old King of Prussia*, 1887
92. Princes Parade, pre-1909
93. Ballards Lane, 1899
94. Tally Ho Corner, 1896
95. Tally Ho Corner, c.1919
96. East Finchley station, c.1925
97. Grays Bros., coal merchants, 1927
98. Tram car 115 at East Finchley, c.1905
99. High Road East Finchley, c.1904-5
100. Huntingdon Road in the early 1900s
101. High Road East Finchley, c.1910
102. Creighton Avenue, c.1901
103. High Road at Squires Lane, c.1905
104. East Weald, c.1911
105. East End Road, 1905
106. All Saints' church, Friern Barnet, c.1920
107. Iron chapel, East End Road
108. St Mary's R.C. chapel
109. High Road Whetstone at Green Road, c.1880
110. High Road Whetstone at Friern Barnet Lane, c.1890
111. Harper's bakery, c.1890
112. Bell Cottages, c.1905
113. The Catchpole family outside Bell Cottages, 1896
114. The Sailor's Home Refreshment Rooms, c.1920
115. Woodhouse Lane, c.1908
116. Goldsmith Road, c.1915
117. The Parade, Friern Barnet Road, 1906
118. Friern Barnet Road at Station Road, c.1904
119. Laying the Friern Barnet sewer, c.1895
120. Laying the Finchley sewer, c.1900-10
121. Finchley fire brigade station in the 1930s
122. Friern Avenue Laundry, c.1905
123. Finchley Skating Rink, c.1910
124. The Picturedrome, c.1912
125. The Bohemia, c.1915
126. The *Railway Hotel*, c.1909
127. East Finchley Cricket Club, 1893
128. East End Road, c.1900
129. Sanger's Circus auction of 1903
130. Nether Court
131. East Finchley Board school, c.1912
132. St Michael's Convent school
133. The laboratory at the Convent School of Marie Auxiliatrice in the 1930s
134. Finchley Guide, c.1905
135. Finchley Cottage Hospital fund-raising committee, 1905
136. Finchley Cottage Hospital, 1908
137. Finchley Carnival, c.1907
138. Finchley Carnival, c.1907
139. Victoria Park, c.1902
140. Friary Park, c.1910
141. Avenue House
142. Woodside Hall sale catalogue of 1905
143. Stephens Memorial Hall
144. King Edward Hall during the First World War
145. The temporary hospital during the First World War
146. Nurses sewing during the First World War
147. Northern Junction Railway Menace, 1913
148. Jackson's coal wharf, c.1917
149. *The Cricketers*, 1900
150. *The Cricketers* and Nether Street, 1920
151. Friern Watch Estate sale catalogue of the 1920s
152. Chandos Avenue in the 1920s
153. High Road Whetstone, c.1923
154. Lawson's timber merchants, Whetstone
155. Watercress beds, c.1910
156. Junction of the North Circular Road and Falloden Way, 1933
157. Unveiling of *La Delivrance* in 1927
158. *Manor Cottage Tavern*, c.1912
159. Car outing to Brighton in 1924
160. Tollhouse at *Spaniards*, 1935
161. Bus on the forecourt of *The Griffin*, 1927
162. Kingsway tram terminus, 1935
163. Frenchman's Gusset in the early 20th century
164. Brook Farm, 1914
165. Oakleigh Park Farm
166. Jersey Farm Dairies advertisement, c.1900
167. Floats of the Farm Dairies Ltd., c.1936/7
168. Cow house, College Farm, c.1910
169. The stack yard, College Farm, 1893
170. Argyle Road, 1900
171. Lily Mortimer, Finchley's last shepherdess in 1934
172. Ingleway, 1921
173. Red Lion Hill, 1938
174. Grange estate under construction, 1938
175. Oak Lane health centre
176. Windermere Avenue, 1932
177. Etchingham Court, c.1935
178. Finchley open-air pool, 1931
179. North Finchley library, 1936
180. Gaumont opening souvenir brochure, 1937
181. The Priory and Friern Barnet Town Hall, 1940
182. The 393 (Finchley) Squadron Air Training Corps, 1941
183. Victory celebrations at Avenue House grounds, 1945

Acknowledgements

Finchley and Friern have always inspired great interest and affection, and the local collection is constantly enriched by the contributions of many local historians and enthusiasts. Amongst these we should like to acknowledge particularly C. O. Banks, Nicholas Benn, W. Colbert, Fred Davis, Irene Dawson, the Finchley Society, Andrew Forsyth, Judith Grant, Arthur Hall, John Heathfield, M. C. Moore, Herbert Norman, David Paul, Jack Prime, A. J. Pryor, Percy Reboul, Dave Ruddom, Cyril Smeeton and H. H. Wilmot.

Users and curators of the collection are also constantly aware of their debt to the authors of the chapters on Friern and Finchley in the *Victoria County History of Middlesex*, Volume VI, which since its publication in 1980 has been the indispensable reference book for the history of the area.

Despite all the help we are bound to have made mistakes, and there are still obvious gaps in the collection. Anyone who can help remedy our inevitable sins of omission or commission will benefit many future users of the Archives & Local Studies Centre.

Illustration Acknowledgements

The authors wish to thank the following for the use of illustrations: Nicholas Benn, 13, 28, 131, 158; Andrew Forsyth, 75, 90, 145; Grace English, 148; Friern Hospital, 57; Judith Grant, 132; John Heathfield, 39; W. Noel Jackson, 161; David Paul, 72a, 77, 116, 152; Percy Reboul, 83, 109, 112-14, 154, 165. The rest of the illustrations come from the collections of Barnet Libraries' Archives & Local Studies Centre.

Introduction

The early history of both Finchley and Friern is very obscure. There have been a few stray stone-and bronze-age finds but not enough to prove that there was any regular settlement either before or during the Roman period. Almost the whole area is heavy clay soil, on which grew thick forest. Since this was difficult both to clear and to plough, and the soil was in any case fairly infertile, sparse early occupation is unsurprising.

We do not know when the first real settlements were made. Both Finchley and Barnet are Anglo-Saxon place-names, but probably late ones. Finchley means a clearing either by Finch or of finches, while Barnet may well mean a clearing by burning. The first Barnet settlement was in any case what is now East Barnet, and Friern was almost certainly later. We cannot even be completely sure that Finchley and Friern were in existence by 1066: Anglo-Saxon words continued to be used for place-names for some time after the Norman Conquest and, worse still, neither Finchley nor any of the Barnets is named in Domesday Book. This absence is not conclusive, though. Domesday Book was arranged by administrative units, not villages or settlements, and Finchley and Friern may already have been included, as they certainly were later, within the Bishop of London's great manor of Fulham.

Regular references to Finchley and Friern begin in the late 12th century, which is the time when written records become more frequent. Archaeological findings, however, point the same way. Most of the pottery found at a recent dig at Church End Finchley, came from the period 1150-1250, although a few sherds were earlier. Both the parish churches, St Mary at Finchley and St James' Friern Barnet, seem to date from the late 12th century. Whatever may have happened earlier, the continuous history of this area, at the level of both overlordship and settlement, traces back to that period.

The Bishop of London was the manorial overlord of the whole area until the 1190s when, after buying out his previous tenant, he gave his Barnet land to the religious order of the Hospitallers – hence the subsequent adjective of Friern, meaning belonging to the Friars or Brothers. At the Reformation Friern passed to the chapter of St Paul's Cathedral. As always, other sub-manors or freehold estates also developed within the manor. The most important was Halliwick, which was created in the 13th century and was sometimes called the manor of Colney Hatch.

Although the Bishops of London retained Finchley, the manorial demesne land – or home farm – was always granted out, and became the sub-manor of Bibbesworth. This was bought and sold by a succession of city merchants, gentry and aristocrats until 1622 when a city alderman, Edward Allen, bought it and established a family interest which lasted until the lands were finally sold off for development. The manor house on East End Road, an 18th-century rebuild, survived and today houses the Sternberg Centre.

For all its difficulties, the area's heavy woodland was a valued resource, providing the timber, grazing, charcoal and tanning vital to a pre-Industrial Revolution economy. By the early 13th century the Bishops of London had created a large enclosed park within their adjoining manors of Hornsey and Finchley. The toll gate at *Spaniards* commemorates its western edge, and the gate house at Highgate its southern, while Cherry Tree Woods are a remaining portion at its northern limit. Although long disemparked, the original boundary of Hornsey Park could still easily be traced on 19th-century maps.

North of the park was Finchley Wood, later Finchley Common. Rights in this, as in all the woods in Finchley, Friern and Hornsey, were shared – and regularly disputed – between the residents of all three. The Common was denuded of trees by the end of the 18th century, but was only finally enclosed in 1816. This was the only formal enclosure within the area since it had never had the large open fields of the Midlands arable belt. Some slight experience of what the Common must once have felt like can still be gained in the Glebelands and Coppetts Wood Nature Reserve.

The wood and underlying heavy soil determined the settlement pattern; instead of the large nucleated villages of the open field areas there was a number of small hamlets. These were always sited on high land since the combination of a high water table, many streams and rivulets, and poor drainage made dryness the main criterion. By the 14th century, as well as the original settlement at Church End Finchley, there were others at East End and North End, or East Finchley and the western side of Whetstone. East Finchley in fact had two: East End itself, centred around Market Place and extending along East End Road, and Park Gate. The actual gate was in the dip where the *White Lion* and the station now are, but it is clear from maps that the settlement was up the hill, at the junction of the Great North Road with East End Road and Fortis Green. Over time other hamlets also developed, particularly Woodside, Fallow Corner and Cuckolds Haven, all at the Common's western edge. Their sites today are marked by Woodside Lane, Finchley Hospital and the Grange estate at Red Lion Hill.

Friern was much more thinly populated. The original settlement was probably by the church but moved up to Whetstone, whose name almost certainly reflects this westward move; certainly since it is recorded by 1398 it has nothing to do with the legendary use of the stone outside *The Griffin* as a whetstone by soldiers sharpening their swords en route to the Battle of Barnet in 1471. There was also a medieval hamlet at Colney Hatch. Betstile is an early road junction, and a field there was recorded in 1390, but it was only very sparsely settled until the 19th century, when it became known as New Southgate.

All the settlements were linked by various lanes and paths, and before motor transport there was no absolute distinction between roads and footways. Most survive, although Ducksetters Lane, the original road from Church End Finchley to Temple Fortune, has vanished completely. All our named lanes are early connecting routes, as are the long-distance paths which never became roads. Among these are Church Path, which linked Whetstone to Nether Street and thus to St Mary's at Church End, and The Walks, linking East End and Cuckolds Haven via Bow Lane to Fallow Corner. At suburbanisation most of the lanes lost their distinctive character and, as earlier, sometimes changed their names. Oakleigh Road North conceals the medieval route to Wood Green and Edmonton known at various times as Avernstreet, Hungerdown, Blackhorse Lane and Station Road. Some early paths became hidden within new roads, for instance Granville Road which links Fallow Corner to Ballards Lane. Ballards Lane and Nether Street were an early extension from Church End, and indeed together form one of the standard medieval village street plans.

The economic advantages of the area's abundant woodland were enhanced by two other important factors. One was proximity to London, and the other the siting of the new medieval Great North Road. The main Roman routes, Watling and Ermine Streets, skirt the Northern Heights and thus pass either side of the area, but a completely new main road was created in the late 11th or early 12th century. The original route came up through Muswell Hill, Colney Hatch and Friern Barnet Lanes, turning at what is now Whetstone towards Chipping Barnet and St Albans. Then in the late 13th or early 14th century the Bishop of London allowed a new road to be put through his park between Highgate and East Finchley, and the connecting stretch through Finchley Wood was soon built.

Even the road could not attract dwellers into Finchley Wood, and 18th-century maps still show only one small settlement within the Common, at Brownswells where Norden had found a well 'late re-edified' for travellers in 1593. Settlements at the Common's edge, however, benefited greatly. As mentioned above, the original settlement at Friern, which lay on the first route of the Great North Road, probably moved up to the new junction soon after it was created, thus forming the eastern side of Whetstone. Although Church End Finchley neither moved nor stagnated, its daughter settlements at North End (such as Whetstone) and East End grew faster.

From the arrival of the Great North Road (or High Road) until the invention of the railways in the 1830s the area was closely involved in providing for the needs of travellers and of the city itself. These needs expanded over time, and particularly after the 18th-century Agricultural and Industrial Revolutions brought enormous growth, both in the city's population and in long-distance travel. The road was under a turnpike trust from 1712 until 1862, with local toll gates at East Finchley and Whetstone. The removal of tolls caused enormous local rejoicing. Inns and smithies flourished, and there was a particular concentration at Whetstone.

Carriers carting local or more distant hay into London (whose horses were as insatiable as its citizens), and soot and manure out again, caused what is now the *White Lion* at East Finchley to be known as the *Dirthouse*. Grass, at first for grazing but then primarily for hay, replaced any local arable crops. Meat for London could only keep fresh on the hoof, and drovers from ever further afield brought their animals to markets on London's periphery, sited where there was plentiful grazing. Market Place, the original centre of East Finchley, hosted a celebrated twice-weekly pig market by the early 18th century.

The combination of the road and the Common was also appreciated by highwaymen. Finchley Common was notorious as the haunt of Jack Shepherd and Dick Turpin, but much of this was legendary. Robberies were indeed frequent but were mostly carried out by lesser-known local residents. They were ultimately stopped by mounted patrols, set up around London in 1805, and by the Common's enclosure in 1816. The enclosure also removed an open space which had been used intermittently for a number of other activities, ranging from troop encampments through sporting fixtures and duels to, probably, early dissenters' meetings. Local Nonconformists though, had developed ordinary, and successful, meeting houses well before 1816.

In 1825 work began on a new turnpike road from St Marylebone to the Great

North Road. Known further south as the Finchley Road, its local sections were the new Regents Park Road, which replaced the differently aligned Ducksetter's Lane and bypassed Church End to run straight into an improved Ballards Lane. The new junction at Tally Ho (to which Ballards Lane had to be slightly extended) became an important focal point for future development, even after the coming of the railways in the 1830s abruptly ended the coaching era.

The first railway to pass through the area was the Great Northern line to York, which opened with a station then called Colney Hatch, now New Southgate, in 1850. The station was provided primarily for the second Middlesex County Pauper Lunatic Asylum, now Friern Hospital, which opened the following year. Both provided new local employment, and cheap housing sprang up in New Southgate. In the 1860s development of the Freehold (South Friern) was precipitated by an influx of labourers working on Alexandra Palace.

Elsewhere, and before the arrival of the suburban lines and commuter housing, there were other developments. The scale of brickmaking and building increased. Considerable numbers of new cottages enlarged Whetstone, East End and Woodside. Cottages also began to be built on the newly-enclosed Common, particularly on the strip west of the High Road at North Finchley, with developments such as Lodge Lane and Frederick's Place. There were also some new villas, as well as cottages, on various stretches of the High Road.

The collapse of coaching weakened the local economy, but new ways arose to serve the ever-expanding capital and its needs. Market gardens began to appear: the first in Ballards Lane in 1845, and among others James Sweet's at Whetstone, opened in about 1862; as the nurseries expanded they became major local employers. Also in Whetstone Joseph Baxendale, owner of Pickfords carriers, built Woodside, plus a hospital for 100 sick horses. He also donated the site for St John's church and school, which were opened respectively in 1832 and 1833 on the Finchley side. This was the first new Anglican building to supplement the two original medieval parish churches, and thus to begin to challenge the various Nonconformist meetings which were already active throughout the area.

At East End a plan to build a large reservoir at Strawberry Vale when Finchley Common was enclosed failed (so that the Welsh Harp fell instead to Hendon), but other large open spaces which also carried employment opportunities were created. The St Pancras and Islington cemeteries opened in 1854, followed the next year by the St Marylebone cemetery, and ornamental stone masonry flourished accordingly. The hog market was still held in 1845, but had gone by 1869. While it continued, the confinement imposed by the Common's enclosure plus the increase of housing around Market Place contributed to many sanitary and social problems in the area. Methodists and Congregationalists were already established, and the latter founded a school in Chapel Street in 1842. Many better-off residents were increasingly concerned about both the social conditions and the Nonconformist activity, and lobbying led by the Salvin family resulted in Holy Trinity church and school, both designed by Anthony Salvin, opening in 1846-7. The latter was specifically designed to give vocational training to the poor: animal husbandry for the boys and domestic service for the girls.

This had always been an area of social contrast since its advantages as a rural location with easy access to London had been obvious to the wealthy. Large houses began to spread up Ballards Lane and Nether Street and along East End Road from the late Middle Ages onwards, and Colney Hatch too became very much a gentlemen's enclave. Villa residences were built in the early 19th century, including some within the newly-enclosed Common, which were designed to appeal to those who owned their own carriages or, if they lived conveniently for the coaching routes, could afford to use the coaches. Various private schools were opened, including one at Finchley (Bibbesworth) Manor House. This closed shortly after Finchley's rector started what became Christ's College in 1857.

Many of these wealthier residents could be described as the first commuters, but their journeys to the city might well have been infrequent. By the 1860s both the railway companies and developers hoped to change this by opening up the area to daily travellers. There were numerous abortive schemes from 1861 onwards, but the eventual outcome was a line which opened in 1867 coming overland from Finsbury Park through East End, Church End and Mill Hill to Edgware. A branch beyond Church End through Woodside Park (until 1882 Torrington Park) and Totteridge to High Barnet opened in 1872. It was only in 1939 that the line was connected by a tunnel from East Finchley to Archway and the older route discontinued, as was passenger traffic beyond Mill Hill East. In 1873 Oakleigh Park station was opened on the main line, and in 1933 West Finchley on the High Barnet branch. In 1886 local residents, presumably mostly newly-arrived commuters, who disliked the connotations of the name East End, successfully petitioned for East End (Finchley) station's name to be changed to East Finchley, and the new name soon ousted the old for the whole area. Finchley (Church End) station did not become Finchley Central until 1940.

Few of these stations were ideally placed, and the suburban line's initial route into London was slow and inconvenient. Buses provided little additional help until the 1890s. Developers may also have been over-optimistic about commuters' desire to live so far out while there were still new areas becoming available further in towards town. The maps, sales catalogues and newspapers of the next 50 years, and the evidence of our eyes today, all tell the same tale: there was some development certainly, but far less than both optimists and pessimists had predicted. All the old settlements expanded and a new centre at North Finchley and Woodside Park emerged, but the intervening fields were not yet submerged.

There was a curious quirk at East Finchley, where some roads were developed simultaneously with the railway, but apparently not for commuters. They were at the maximum point from any station, in the block of land between East End Road, Long Lane, Church Lane and (now) the North Circular, and the houses were mostly modest cottages. The land must simply have become available and been seized by builders already active in extending the spread of cottages in the Church Lane and Cuckolds Haven area. A big local petition in 1892 for a more convenient station, to be sited either at Manor Cottages or where Bishop Douglass school now is, was dismissed by the railway company because such a station would not generate more custom.

One unique development was The Bishop's Avenue, where the road was put through the heart of the former Hornsey Park in about 1887, and the building of houses for the notably rich began in 1894. Famous residents have included Gracie Fields and Evelyn Waugh's Lord Copper, and for a while 'East Finchley' for the rest of the world meant The Bishop's Avenue. Apart from land let to the Hampstead Golf Club, the rest of the land west of The Bishop's Avenue was leased in 1909 and 1911 for the extension of Hampstead Garden Suburb. A few houses were quickly built, but the main development occurred between the wars. Hampstead Garden Suburb was not the only local result of the garden city and co-partnership movements, which also inspired both Finchley and Brent Garden Villages.

The expansion was not confined to houses. Shops were becoming increasingly important, and Ballards Lane and the High Road at East and North Finchley in particular were transformed into new-style shopping centres. The centre of Church End shifted, appropriately enough, from the church to the station and Broadway. Only Whetstone High Road was little affected, until the full development of its surrounding area between the wars. New horse-drawn bus routes appeared in the 1890s, and the first motor bus began in 1905. In the same year the Metropolitan Electric Tramways line opened from Highgate to Whetstone, and was extended to the Hertfordshire county boundary in 1906 and Chipping Barnet in 1907. From 1909 it was crossed by one from New Southgate to Finchley and Golders Green. The tramway depot which opened in 1905 just behind Tally Ho became the focus of the M.E.T.'s system. The coming of the tram tracks, and then the removal of the original poles to the sides of the streets in 1913-14, are an important help in dating many early street scenes.

Churches and chapels, schools, social halls and sports facilities also appeared, all providing new community links for new communities as well as specific services. For many this was the classic pre-1914 golden age. The glow should not, however, obscure the rest of the picture. Many ventures, both high-minded and purely commercial, were short-lived; among the former, the Athenaeum Institution, which opened in Oakleigh Park in 1881 and hoped to promote social, artistic and scientific interests, survived barely a decade, enriching posterity only by its name.

The deprivation in all the old poor areas, Whetstone, East Finchley, New Southgate and South Friern, continued unabated, and where new and old residents lived nearby there cannot have been overmuch social integration. There was no longer any timelag in the provision of Nonconformist and Anglican facilities, and in the poorer areas both functioned as mission churches, with soup kitchens a regular necessity. The battle over education was grimly fought; the number of places available in the Anglican and Nonconformist schools was not enough, and the churches and chapels did not have sufficient funds to meet the expanding need. The Anglicans, unlike the Nonconformists, nevertheless strongly resisted the introduction of school boards which would supply non-denominational schools. In Finchley a school board was finally established in 1881, but the resistance in Friern was successful until the 1902 Education Act. After this Finchley's school board became part of Finchley U.D.C., while Friern's primary education became a Middlesex County Council responsibility.

There were other facilities which neither voluntary nor commercial initiatives could provide. Both Finchley and Friern Barnet vestries were almost always more scared of the prospect of spending ratepayers' money than of the consequences of failing to do so, so that only the very real threat of cholera finally forced them to adopt proper sewerage systems – Finchley in the late 1860s and Friern in the 1880s. In Finchley the vestry was replaced by a Local Board in 1878, but there were no wards so that it was effectively controlled by Church End, the most wealthy but least populous district. In 1881 the board rejected a suggested union with Friern, which established its own Local Board in 1884. Wards were successfully achieved in Friern in 1888, but in Finchley it took another decade, and was achieved only after both boards had become Urban District Councils in 1895. Disputes over the provision of services continued, and many were achieved later than elsewhere.

The inter-war years saw the final transformation into suburbia. The farms and fields vanished, ending a highly successful period of dairy farming, and the Dollis Brook was channelled. Most of the older large houses too vanished, as did some of the cottages. The new housing which replaced them was somewhat more uniform but still highly attractive to those migrating from London's centre or East End. Notable among the newcomers to Finchley, if not to Friern, were the number of Jewish families. The first Jewish families had arrived in the 1910s and early 1920s and settled in the Church End and Woodside Park areas, but it was not until the 1930s that their numbers grew significantly and their centre of gravity moved southward towards the newly-developed Finchley part of Hampstead Garden Suburb and the new estates bordering Golders Green. The first purpose-built synagogues appeared in these areas, the Hampstead Garden Suburb Synagogue at Norrice Lea opening in 1934 and the Finchley Synagogue at Kinloss Gardens opening the following year.

At the same time new trunk roads were driven through the area, thus temporarily helping to alleviate the new problems caused by mass car ownership while also providing some relief for the period's heavy unemployment. During the 1920s the North Circular was built, and the Great North Road ceased to be the main road to the north, with traffic diverted west up Falloden Way to the new Great North Way. As well as cars other wider changes had an obvious local impact: trolley-buses replaced trams in 1936-8; new cinemas, notably the Gaumont at Tally Ho which opened in 1939, augmented earlier ones.

Perhaps the biggest change was the more active approach adopted by the local councils. By 1930 housing was Finchley's chief expense, followed by electric lighting. In the following decade there was some slum clearance, and condemned cottages in both Whetstone and East Finchley were demolished as A.R.P. (Air Raid Precaution) practice. At the same time the council began to provide libraries, health centres, and more open spaces, and built the open-air pool. Friern Council's activities were on a smaller scale but it too provided housing, and more open spaces; its libraries were provided by the county.

The councils' activities were recognised as essential, and helped to foster local identification in areas which were undergoing very rapid change. There was much local rejoicing when Finchley became a Municipal Borough in 1933, with associated ceremonies of considerable pomp. Two years later Friern fought off becoming included within it. When war came the stronger councils with their greater public support were ready and able to lead the local war effort, taking responsibility for civil defence and spearheading a range of fund-raising and sponsoring activities. The victory celebrations in 1945 were genuine civic events.

These celebrations mark the cut-off point for this book. The post-war period has of course seen the usual mixture of gradual development and sudden change, and some continuing trends produced more drastic results. The old centre of East Finchley was demolished as slum clearance by the council in the early 1960s, and the high-rise parts of the replacement became landmarks for a considerable area. Whetstone High Road, already much changed in the inter-war years, has received a particular concentration of new offices, again including high-rise. Under the London Government Act of 1963 the new London Borough of Barnet was formed in 1965 and included both Finchley and Friern, while the old county of Middlesex disappeared. One considerable post-war change has been the great diversity of new residents, and Finchley and Friern are now among the most ethnically mixed parts of London, with the fabric of local life enriched by strands from almost every part of the world.

Despite all the changes – and change, after all, is nothing new – local loyalties remain strong. For their residents the various hamlets and areas are as distinct, and unique, as they have always been. It is hoped that this book will strengthen understanding and enjoyment of our past, and therefore of our present. Most of the sources used come from the borough's Archives and Local Studies Centre, which has many more and is always happy to welcome all enquirers.

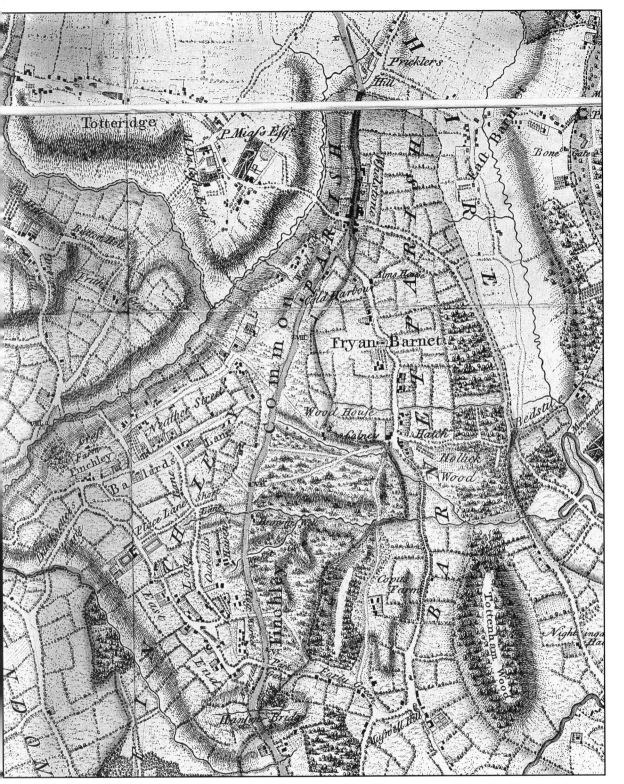

1. Rocque's survey of 1754 is the first detailed map of the area, and a clear guide to its essential features. The sheer size of Finchley Common is immediately striking. The pattern of the settlements and their interconnecting lanes is also plain, and can still be discerned today, underlying more recent developments.

2 & 3. Two views of the Dollis Brook, which formed Finchley's western boundary. The viaduct carrying a stretch of the railway line between Finchley Central and Mill Hill East opened in 1867. A little further south, the long ford vanished soon after this picture was taken in 1904, when the river was culverted beneath the road.

4 & 5.   Beating the bounds. The annual perambulation of the parish boundaries to fix them in the community's memory was originally led by the parish priest. Here the tradition is being carried on by the parishes' civil successors, Friern Barnet U.D.C. in 1910, and most enthusiastically by Finchley Borough Council shortly after receiving its Charter of Incorporation in 1933. The mayor is being 'bumped' on the boundary line.

6 & 7. The 12th-century south doorway to St James Friern Barnet was the only part of the original church to survive the 1853 rebuilding. As these views from 1779 and 1892 show, it has long been hidden from the outside by an entry porch.

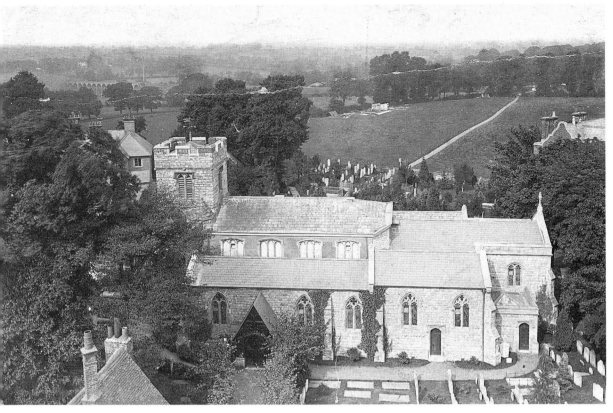

8 & 9. St Mary at Finchley around the end of the century. The church has been frequently altered since its 12th-century foundation, and the east end seen here was lost after bombing in 1940.

10.   Finchley or Bibbesworth Manor House was rebuilt in the 18th century, leaving no trace of its medieval predecessor. This had been moated, but the rectangle of water beside Squires Lane partly shown here, though called The Moat, was a later fish pond. A favourite spot for children, fishermen and others, it was built over in *c*.1905.

11.   The Avenue connected the manor house and parish church, and was planted with trees by the lady of the manor in about 1604. Long afterwards it gave its name to Avenue House.

12.   There was no manor house at Friern Barnet until shortly after the Reformation when the new lords of the manor, the Chapter of St Paul's Cathedral, ordered their tenant to build one. This became known, understandably but misleadingly, as The Friary or Friern House. Seen here in 1797, it was replaced in the 19th century by the present house, standing in what is now Friary Park. The building north of the church which was called Manor or Manor House Farm was never any sort of a manor house.

13.   Cherry Tree Wood once formed the northern part of Hornsey Park, the Bishop of London's medieval hunting park. It did not become a public park until purchased by the Council in 1915. These children with their pram and soft toys are captured on a postcard sent in 1926.

14.   Railway Cottages stood at the junction of East End Road and The Causeway, and long predated the railway. Although The Causeway passes the back of East Finchley station, it originated as a path up from the exit of the Bishop of London's park, near the *White Lion*. The cottages were demolished in 1971.

15.   The view south from the corner of The Bishop's Avenue in *c*.1905. The large house in the distance marks Finchley's boundary with Hornsey. The Bishop of London allowed this stretch of the Great North Road to be put through his park between Highgate and East Finchley in about 1300. The Bishop's Avenue (the signpost points to Hampstead and Kilburn) was put through in about 1887.

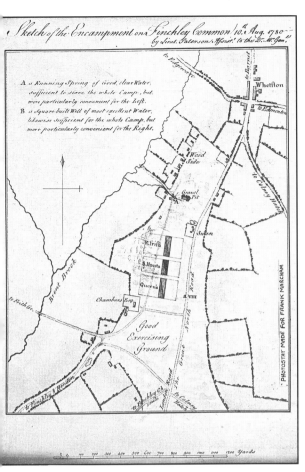

A a Running Spring of Good, clear Water, sufficient to serve the whole Camp, but more particularly convenient for the Left.

B a Square-built Well of most excellent Water, likewise Sufficient for the whole Camp, but more particularly convenient for the Right.

16.   Once Finchley Common had lost its trees it was ideal for military training, as this sketch of a 1780 encampment illustrates. It also underlines the absence of settlement on the Common, most notably at the junction which became Tally Ho, in contrast to the development at Whetstone and Wood- (or Common-)side.

17.   The tradition that John Bunyan and Richard Baxter held meetings on Finchley Common after the imposition of religious restrictions in the 1660s is recorded in this 1847 print. Nonconformity was certainly strong throughout the area.

Dick Turpin's Oak, Finchley Comm

18 & 19. Turpin's Oak on the corner of Oak Lane was a celebrated, or notorious, landmark on the Great North Road crossing Finchley Common. After the coaching era numerous pistol balls, fired either by highwaymen testing their weapons or by coach drivers as a deterrent, were extracted from its trunk. The top sketch is undated but supplies an interesting early view of the area as well as the tree. By 1873, when the lower photograph was taken, the oak lay within the grounds of Hilton House. It was obviously already decaying, and was finally removed in 1952.

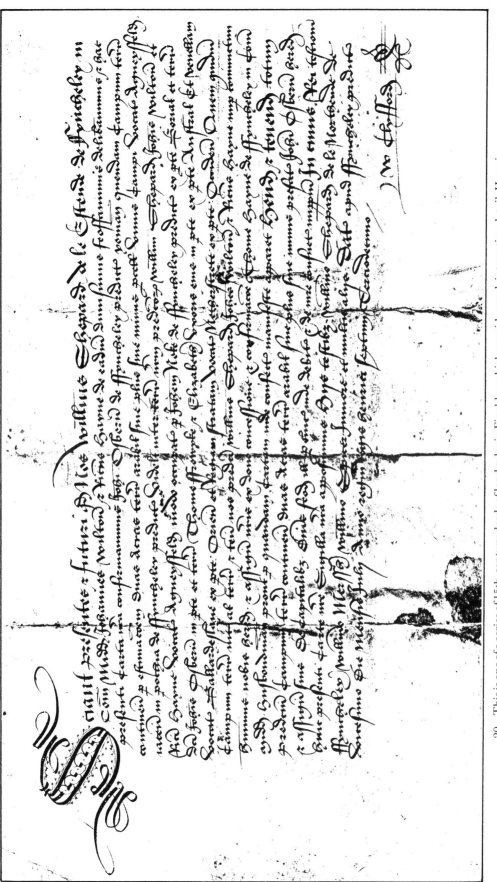

20. This is one of a series of 15th-century deeds of land sales in Finchley which provide much interesting detail. Here, in 1498, William Shepard, John Wilton and Richard Hayne 'de le Estende de Fyncheley' sell John Osbern a two-acre field called Agneysfeld lying between Ballards Lane and Nether Street.

21.   The Shepard and Hayne families recur in the early history of the Finchley parish charities, whose first donations were received in 1488-9. The first almshouses were 'lately built' on part of Pointalls in East Finchley in 1612, in accordance with the will of John Hayne. These were replaced in 1739 by the cottages seen here, which were in turn replaced in 1895 by the new building visible in the background. This is now the oldest part of the much extended development known as Wilmot Close.

22.   The Campe almshouses in Friern Barnet Lane were endowed by Lawrence Campe, a London merchant, in 1610-12. Much of the original buildings remain, although the founder's strict conditions about religious observance have long been abandoned.

23. The area was not well covered by print makers, and some scenes, such as this 'cottage near Finchley' of 1779, seem to be purely imaginary.

24. King John's general charter to the Bishop of London giving all his tenants freedom from tolls probably explains the legends of a more specific local connection with this not normally popular king. He was supposed to have lived in this house – King John's House in King Street, seen here shortly before its demolition in 1904 – and also in the 19th-century King John's Cottages nearby in Long Lane.

25. The *Green Man* was part of the solitary small settlement actually on Finchley Common: an oasis at Brownswells. By the time this early 20th-century photograph was taken the inn had been substantially refaced, but it was demolished and replaced in 1935. The replacement is currently scheduled for demolition when the North Circular is widened.

26. The burglary at Farmer Daniel Clewin's house in 1778 attracted what today seems an amazing amount of attention. It occurred at The Hill House in Cuckolds Haven, one of the early settlements on the western edge of Finchley Common.

27. Another 18th-century house at Cuckolds Haven was Oak Lodge. Edward Sayer, a prominent local figure, bought it in 1861 and built The Grange next door in 1863. Oak Lodge, seen here in 1947, became a Special School in 1916. The school moved to Heath View in 1973 and the house, by now within the CAV Lucas factory site, was demolished in the 1980s.

28. The Grange remained a private house until the First World War. In 1919 it briefly became a piano factory before passing in 1920 to Simms Motor Units. Simms was one of the major pioneers of the British motor industry, and new factory buildings soon spread around the original house. After being merged with CAV Lucas in 1968, the factory closed in 1991.

29a & b.   The Goodyear family at Fallow Lodge in about 1870. Fallow Lodge, later Holdenhurst, was one of the main houses at Fallow Corner, the commonside settlement at the top of Bow Lane in existence since at least the 15th century. Holdenhurst was demolished in c.1905, when Holdenhurst and Chislehurst Avenues were built. Another resident of Fallow Corner, from 1806-1827, was the famous clown Joseph Grimaldi, who is commemorated by a plaque near the site of his house, on the Granville Road wall of Finchley Hospital.

30. Grimaldi's memoirs were edited by Charles Dickens, who is said to have stayed here, at Fallow or Cobleys Farm on the southern corner of Bow Lane, while writing *Martin Chuzzlewit* in 1843. The farm covered some 80 acres between Ballards, Long, Squires and Bow Lanes until residential development began in the 1880s. This started slowly, but by the time the house was demolished in *c.*1905 it had outlived most of its fields.

31. The Whetstone stretch of Russell Lane was also known as East Barnet Lane, which highlights the point that most lanes are early connecting routes. When it was built up, between the wars, part of one side became a central strip, thus preserving something of the original character.

32. Squires Lane, pictured with its Edwardian terraces in 1907, seems an ordinary suburban street. In fact it had a long history as a link from East End Road at the Manor House to the Great North Road, and it was not suburbanised until this period.

33. The view down Swan Lane in the 1930s. The late Victorian cottages on the right went in the early 1970s but two pairs of early 19th-century cottages further on at North Place remain. North Place became the point at which the lane, which connects Whetstone to Woodside, shrank to a footpath.

34. Coppetts Farm was cleared from the woodland in the 16th century, and until the mid-19th century was the only building in Friern Barnet south of the Bounds Brook – or North Circular. The 1670 farmhouse shown here lingered on at the end of Wilton Road until the mid-1930s.

The Woodhouse Finchley Middlesex as it was in 1797.

35 & 36. The history of Woodhouse –
in the 17th century three 'wood
houses' – is very complicated. In 1765
it was inherited by the wife of the
celebrated plasterer, Thomas Collins
Although the house was largely
reconstructed in 1888, some of Collins'
plasterwork was spared. The building
became Woodhouse Grammar School
(now a Sixth Form College) in 1925.

37. Coldharbour was the area of Whetstone just below today's Green Road, and in the 18th century was an important centre for horse trading. This house, also known as Coldharbour, was built on part of the land in the mid-18th century and was at one stage an inn, known as the *Dog* and then the *Queen's Head*. Next to it northwards was the house known both as Coldharbour House and as Woodlands, which around 1914 became an early film studio. The whole site was redeveloped in the 1950s.

38. Whetstone, *c*.1880. The bowler-hatted gent is resting his foot on the famous 'whetstone'. Behind it is the village post office, next to which, partially obscured by the tree, is *The Griffin* inn before its 1920's rebuild. The tree disappeared along with others which had lined the High Road when pavements began to be provided from the 1890s.

39. Recent investigation of the back extension behind the old post office has revealed a Tudor timber-framed building previously hidden under later coverings. The frontage is now probably 18th century, but there are traces of *c*.1500 materials in the similar frontage to its north.

40.   Almost opposite, standing in the road by the southern corner of Totteridge Lane, stood the Whetstone tollhouse. The Great North Road was freed of tolls in 1862 and this picture was taken during the demolition of the gate in October 1863. The house survived a few years longer.

41.   The Finchley Road was built from 1825 as a turnpike road to link the West End to the Great North Road at Tally Ho. It followed an entirely new route from Regents Park to Church End and then used an improved Ballards Lane to Tally Ho. The imposition of tolls along the previously free Ballards Lane met with undying local hostility. This postcard shows the junction of the new and the old roads at Church End in about 1911, one year before Clements Nursery (centre) was closed and King Edward Hall built on the site, changing the scene considerably by blocking the view of Christ's College.

42 & 43. The *Torrington*, originally a coaching inn, has undergone several alterations and rebuilds. The top photograph shows it in the mid-19th century, when it was a G.P.O. receiving office and regular omnibus stop. The bus outside was on its way from Whetstone into town. The bottom postcard shows the pub after its rebuilding in 1900. This building in turn was demolished and replaced by the present one in 1962.

44. The mail coach changing horses at the *White Lion* in 1825. Today's 1938 building replaced the 18th-century coaching inn shown here. This had also been known both as the *Fleur de Lys* and the *Dirthouse*, the latter because of its popularity with carters bringing hay into London and soot and manure out again. It had probably benefited from being next to the tollgate.

45. Up the hill, the *Bald Faced Stag* was opened, illicitly, in the 1730s, but was known until the 1770s as the *Jolly Blacksmith*. It was completely rebuilt soon after this 1878 photograph was taken. The Congregational church with its landmark spire opened that year, and was demolished in 1965. The crossroads here mark the site of the settlement known as Park Gate, even though the actual gate had been, like the turnpike gate, by the *White Lion*.

46 & 47. The heart of East End, sited at the Common's western edge and therefore also west of the High Road. These 19th-century photographs show the view looking north and south from *The George* inn. The hog market had ended and the High Road was developing, but this remained the village centre. It was redeveloped *c*.1960.

48. The Walks form part of an important route linking the settlements on the western edge of Finchley Common. The name attaches only to the footpaths near Market Place, but the route extended northwards at least to Fallow Corner. Both the trees and the cottages shown in this early 20th-century view have now gone.

49. Houses began to spread from East End along East End Road from the 14th century onwards. This is Elmshurst, which probably dated from the late 16th century but was substantially rebuilt. It was the home of the Salvin family from 1833 to 1857, when they were active in establishing Holy Trinity church and school. The house itself was later a boarding school. It was demolished in 1939 and replaced by Elmhurst Crescent and Pulham Avenue.

50. Park House, facing Gravel Hill at Church End, is one of the few survivors of the large old houses which were once numerous in the area. It dates from 1739, but was probably then a rebuild.

51. The main early spread from Church End was along Ballards Lane and Nether Street. Selina Villa on Ballards Lane was built in 1795, replacing an earlier house. Its owner at the time of this print was also the owner of Thorley's Feeding Stuffs and Cattle Cake. The house is another rare survivor, as Cornwall Lodge, but in greatly shrunken grounds.

SELINA VILLA, FINCHLEY, MIDDLESEX, THE RESIDENCE OF JOSEPH THORLEY.

52a & b.   Next to Selina Villa going south was Falkland House. The lifestyle of its owners, the Tate family, in 1894 is perfectly captured here. The house was replaced by Falkland Avenue in the Edwardian period.

53. Immediately south again was Grove House, also known as The White House. Like most of these large houses, it too had replaced an earlier building. The house seen here was bought in 1844 by Henry Stephens, the inventor of modern ink and father of 'Inky' Stephens, the later owner of Avenue House. The Grove was developed on the site in the Edwardian period.

54. Moss Hall certainly existed by the mid-18th century, and probably by the mid-15th. Following this rural auction an attempt at estate development was made in 1830, but without success. With the coming of the railway, development began from 1867, but the house itself survived until 1927.

55. Brent Lodge was described as the last of Finchley's stately homes during the unsuccessful campaign to prevent its demolition in 1962. It was particularly associated with Francis Hamilton, a prominent local benefactor until his death in 1907. Brent Garden Village was built on part of the estate from *c*.1910.

56. The coming of the railway influenced the siting of Colney Hatch Asylum, latterly Friern Hospital, which opened as the Second Middlesex County Pauper Lunatic Asylum in 1851. It became so well known that for a while Colney replaced Bedlam as a general word for mental hospitals. It was transferred to the L.C.C. in 1889 and the N.H.S. in 1948.

COLNEY HATCH LUNATIC ASYLUM,
FROM THE RAILWAY BRIDGE.

57. The hospital provided a lot of local employment, as this scene in the laundry room indicates.

58. The Avenue district developed in the mid-19th century to house workers employed by the hospital and railway, and was always a notoriously poor area. This view along The Avenue towards Homesdale Road was taken shortly before demolition in 1965.

59. Joseph Baxendale, famous for his development of Pickfords, built Woodside in its magnificent grounds in the 1830s. It later became the Woodside Home for Elderly Ladies, and during the Second World War the Special Constabulary used the front room as its station. The whole estate was redeveloped in the 1980s. The picture dates from the mid-19th century.

60. St John's Whetstone was the first new Anglican church within Finchley. Funded by Joseph Baxendale, it opened as a chapel in 1832 and became a parish in 1836. The architect, Blomfield, was probably the then Bishop of London, whose architect son was still a toddler. The larger poster is advertising the Hospital Sunday Fund collection in 1930.

61. After the enclosure of Finchley Common, development began slowly at North Finchley, particularly on the strip west of the High Road. One of the first developers was Charles Jacques, who started to build cottages in Lodge Lane from 1824, including Torrington Cottage for himself. This stands on the corner of Church Path, the ancient commonside route from Whetstone to Nether Street (and thus to Church End); its southernmost section is now hidden in Netherfield Street. This picture dates from 1949.

62. T. Perkins, gardener and florist, shown here in 1886, lived and traded from Winifred Place, on the High Road between Percy Road and Lodge Lane. These mid-19th century cottages were soon afterwards replaced as North Finchley developed as a shopping centre.

63. North Finchley Congregational church sprang from a local tea merchant's concern in the 1830s for the welfare of the cottagers in the area. This photograph of the minister and deacons with their wives was taken *c*.1914.

64. The Congregationalists also took the lead in providing schools in expanding areas; these were the North Finchley Day Schools not long after they opened in Dale Grove in 1864. Nonconformists supported the establishment of School Boards, and the building became a temporary board school from 1881-4. Thereafter it was sold to the Baptists in 1893, later becoming known as Dale Grove Hall.

65. Christ Church, North Finchley began in 1864 as a mission to navvies working on the railway, and building a permanent church began in 1867. Fund-raising was a widespread problem, and may explain why Christ Church never achieved the spire shown on early prints.

66.   Park Place was a premature start for East Finchley's suburban development; the land was sold in 1800 and there were four villas by 1809. This print, published in 1818, may fall short of Hassall's usual standards of accuracy since the villas seem actually to have run in a line along the south side of Fortis Green, and nos. 3-4 were capable of being joined in 1822 to form Park Hall. The building on the left is the *Bald Faced Stag*.

67.   Prospect Place was built in 1825 to link Market Place with East End Road. The bridge necessitated by the coming of the railway in 1867 remains, but the cottages were demolished in the 1950s.

68. When Finchley Common was enclosed the Regents Canal Company intended to build a large reservoir on part of it. The scheme fell through, however, and in 1816 the company sold Strawberry Vale to James Frost. He was a builder and pioneer cement manufacturer, and built the farmhouse and various villas and cottages there. This photograph of the entrance to the estate was taken in the 1860s. Apart from one pair of cottages, the buildings were demolished prior to the construction of the present estate in the 1970s.

69. St Marylebone cemetery was developed on 26 acres of farmland at East End. This drawing accompanied the *Illustrated London News* account of its consecration in March 1855.

70.   The junction of the Great North Road and Church Lane in a picture probably taken in the 1890s. The state of the road surface is noteworthy. Monumental masons and florists catered for the needs of the nearby St Pancras, Islington and St Marylebone cemeteries.

71.   With the growing number of cottages in the area Church Lane became a flourishing small centre. This early 20th-century photograph shows local traders, the Bailess and Whiteman families, presumably about to embark on a day's excursion. Bailess greengrocers were established at Woodbine Cottages, on the corner of Church Lane, but the delivery cart in the background is a reminder that doorstep delivery was an essential part of the shopkeeper's service.

The Finchley Manuals of Industry.

No. I.

COOKING;

OR,

PRACTICAL AND ECONOMICAL TRAINING

FOR THOSE WHO ARE TO BE

SERVANTS, WIVES, AND MOTHERS.

MANAGEMENT OF THE KITCHEN, PLAIN COOKING, BREAD-
MAKING, BAKING, BREWING, PICKLING.
ETC.

PREPARED FOR THE USE OF THE NATIONAL AND INDUSTRIAL
SCHOOLS OF THE HOLY TRINITY, AT FINCHLEY.

Third Edition.

LONDON :
JOSEPH MASTERS, ALDERSGATE STREET,
AND NEW BOND STREET.
MDCCCLI.

FINCHLEY MANUALS OF INDUSTRY.

No. II. GARDENING ; or, Practical and Economical Training, for the Management of a School or Cottage Garden: embracing
a Knowledge of Soils and their Manures—The Art of Draining—
Spade Husbandry—The Cultivation of Esculent Plants—The
Treatment of the Grape-vine, Strawberry, Gooseberry and Currant
Bushes, and Raspberry Canes—The Cottager's Flower Garden,
&c. Price 10d.

No. III. HOUSEHOLD WORK ; or, The Duties of Female
Servants, in Tradesmen's and other Respectable Middle Class
Families, Practically and Economically Illustrated, through the
respective grades of Maid of All Work—House and Parlour Maid
—and Laundry Maid : embracing, not only General Domestic occupation, but the management of the Laundry, in Washing,
Ironing, &c. With many valuable Recipes for facilitating labour
in every department.

72a & b. Holy Trinity church and school opened in 1846-7, both with a strong missionary purpose. It was the siting of the church which caused the earlier Bulls Lane to become Church Lane. The school, in East End Road, was modelled on northern industrial schools, as its manuals show. When the number of suburban residents grew, more conventional education was required, and the industrial section closed in 1877. The school moved to new premises in 1974 but the old buildings remain.

73. Finchley Hall stood immediately north of St Mary's, in the heart of Church End. From 1838 until 1857 it was used as the original *Queen's Head* inn, but the rector then refused to renew the lease and instead founded Christ's College there. It became the Finchley Council offices from 1902 until bombed in 1940. The inn after some temporary relocations became established at its present site on the corner of East End Road.

74. This view of Church End was taken
before the old village pond was filled in
January 1885. Behind it looms the striking
Gothic building of Christ's College, opened
in 1860. By the end of the century it was in
severe difficulty, and joined the state sector
in 1909. Following amalgamation with the
Alder School, it moved in two phases, in 1978
and 1991, to a new site on East End Road.

75. St Mary's, the earliest Anglican school in Finchley, was founded in 1813. This picture was taken on Empire Day about a century later. The school moved away from its Church End site down to Dollis Park in 1990.

76. Station Road was one of the relatively few streets which developed very soon after Church End (now Finchley Central) station opened in 1867. This picture of its cluttered shops, taken c.1910, is still very recognisable.

77.   Crooked Usage, pictured *c.*1913, was originally simply an unnamed bend on Hendon Lane. The line of Hendon Lane was straightened in 1911-12 with the construction of a new section, then known as Finchley Avenue, along the old footpath which had previously linked Finchley Bridge to the lane.

78.   The view across Finchley Bridge towards Hendon before 1897, when the bridge was rebuilt. The weir, but little else, is still recognisable today.

79. Nether Street in the 1900s was still praised for its picturesque aspect and shady elms. As this picture shows, suburban housing was beginning, but the process would not be completed until the inter-war years.

80. The core of Colney Hatch in about 1903. This scene would soon change beyond all recognition, for by 1909 the *Orange Tree* (now the *Grove*) was rebuilt and the adjacent White House demolished. The wall on the right belonged to The Priory, an 18th-century house replaced by Friern Barnet Town Hall in 1941.

81. Vine Cottages in Colney Hatch Lane, pictured in 1903. In 1909 they were badly damaged by fire while being used as a film location, and had to be demolished. Beyond the cottages are the outbuildings of Hillside Farm, and opposite are the gates to the stables of Halliwick Manor House.

82 & 83. Friern Barnet (or St James') National Schools opened in 1853, replacing the 1809 charity school. The building remains but the school moved in 1975 into the enlarged All Saints. The earlier picture, which also shows an advertisement for building plots on the Myddleton Park estate, is c.1905; the classroom scene was captured in the early 1920s.

84 & 85. Glenroy was one of the first houses built on Seymour Road in the late 1890s as part of the development of the Etchingham Park estate. Its much embellished Tudor style is also typical of other developments of this period, such as the Grass Farm estate around Hendon and Dollis Avenues, with its frontage on Hendon Lane shown in the postcard which dates from the early 1900s. The building in the distance is the old lodge house of the estate. Glenroy itself was demolished in 1972 and replaced, again typically, by a block of flats.

86. On a more modest scale, Finchley Garden Village was developed from 1910 as a small garden suburb, with the houses grouped around a green. The village fête has always been an important part of its community life.

FINCHLEY,

"Field Cottage," Ballards Lane,

Within five minutes' walk of Finchley (Church End) Station, on the Branch Line of the G.N.R.

CATALOGUE

OF

ORCHIDS, CONSERVATORY & GREENHOUSE

PLANTS

AND

OUTDOOR EFFECTS

COMPRISING

4 COWS, 2 HEIFERS, 7 HORSES,

Nearly New Brougham,

WAGONETTE, BUGGY, SPRING CART,

TUMBRIL CART, DOUBLE CYLINDER HORSE ROLLER,

Chain Harrows, Hay Drag and other Rakes, Chaff Machines, Pig Troughs, numerous Iron Hurdles, Garden Seat, Roller, Water Barrow, and other effects, which (having sold the Estate)

Will be Sold by Auction, by

Messrs. CHARLES

SPARROW & SON

UPON THE PREMISES, AS ABOVE,

On Monday, April 21st, 1902,

Commencing at TWO o'clock precisely.

87. By 1902 Church End station had been open 35 years, yet only now was the tide of suburban housing and shops becoming irresistible. Field Cottage was rapidly replaced by Princes Avenue.

88 & 89.   These two pictures show the same stretch of The Broadway in *c*.1880 and *c*.1908. In the 1880s Oxley's on the left was the Church End village butcher and the ivy-covered cottage beyond was the village dairy. Robert Watson's Drapery and Furnishers Store was one of the establishments happy to move from older premises nearby into the new purpose-built parade. Fears that better transport would remove shoppers to London were proving unfounded.

90. The view up the fully developed Broadway, shortly before the arrival of the tramline in 1909.

91. The *Old King of Prussia* in 1887, when its proprietor liked to advertise it as 'an old-fashioned roadside hostelrie – one of those places which are getting rarer every day'. By 1897, however, the inn, which was on the southern corner of the Broadway and Dollis Park, had undergone the first of several rebuilds which removed its quaint charm. It was finally incorporated into a new office block in 1965.

92.   Further up Ballards Lane – by the junction of Long Lane – Princes Parade was flourishing by the time of this picture, again taken shortly before the tramline was laid in 1909 and effectively ended the days of the horse bus.

93.   The shopping area never extended much further towards Tally Ho than Princes Parade. Here is the residential stretch in 1899, showing the usual combination of delivery carts and poor road surfaces. The Methodist church on the left had opened in 1879 but the second building did not appear until 1904.

94 & 95.   Members of the Holophote Cycling Club at Tally Ho in 1896. Cycling was then enormously popular (note the range of wheel sizes employed), and many local inns welcomed the various clubs. The later view of the same spot was on a card posted in 1919, and vividly shows the degree of transformation. More change came in 1927 when the *Park Road Hotel* and the cottages behind it were demolished to make way for the new *Tally Ho!* inn. The *Park Road Hotel* itself had been built in the 1850s, but in 1814 one of the cottages was already providing refreshment: it sold gunpowder, shot and beer.

96.   East End (Finchley) station opened in 1867 and was renamed East Finchley in 1886. It was originally on a Great Northern overground line from Finsbury Park, and came under the London and North Eastern Railway, one of the transitional grouping companies, in 1923 – shortly before this picture was taken. The line was integrated into the Northern Line and electrified in 1939, when the old station was replaced by the present building.

97.   Grays Bros. Coal and Coke Merchants had been established next to the station for almost 40 years when this 1927 picture was taken. The original premises (on the left in the previous picture) were demolished in 1938 during the station rebuilding but new ones were provided. These are now part of the recently enlarged car-park.

98. Trams were suggested for Finchley in 1880 but it was not until 1905 that the Metropolitan Electric Tramways opened their route between Highgate Archway and Whetstone. Fares were low and the route was very popular. Car 115, seen here at East Finchley, had a horrific accident in 1906 when it ran out of control on Archway Hill and struck a hearse, pantechnicon, bus, cab, three pedestrians and another tram.

99. The High Road at East Finchley pictured during the laying of the tram tracks in c.1904-5. There were almost no buildings along this stretch until the late 1890s, when the purpose-built shopping area shown here was rapidly developed.

100. One of the new residential streets for which the shops were developed – Huntingdon Road as it looked in the early 1900s.

101. The northern edge of the Victorian suburban development at East Finchley was also more or less the end of the shopping development of this stretch of the High Road. This view looks southwards from Hertford Road in about 1910. The Black Bess Coffee Tavern existed by the mid-1880s, and in the 1920s became the Black Bess Temperance Hotel, but before its demolition in 1965 was known simply as a transport café. The small building beyond it was the Finchley Athenaeum, then a meeting hall, which would soon have a short spell as an early cinema.

102. Slightly further north, Creighton Avenue was cut through Coldfall Woods in 1899 and opened as a convenient public thoroughfare to Muswell Hill in 1901. Housing did not appear until the inter-war years.

103. This *c.*1905 picture of the junction of Squires Lane with the High Road shows the new shopping parade and a prominent advertising board for semi-detached villas in the recently completed Clifton Road. Finchley County School, visible beyond, had opened in 1903. Until the 1920s Squires Lane rather than the North Circular marked the northern edge of East Finchley district.

104. At the opposite edge of East Finchley, development along The Bishop's Avenue began in the 1890s. East Weald, shown here soon after its construction, was built in 1911 for William Park Lyle the sugar refiner. By the 1930s the road was known as 'Millionaires Row' and among its residents were George Sainsbury and Gracie Fields.

105. A view northwards along East End Road in 1905, when the houses in the foreground were recently built and the trees which lined the road still intact. In the distance Causeway Cottages hide the junction with Church Lane. They were demolished *c*.1960 for a projected road widening.

EAST END ROAD, EAST FINCHLEY.

106. From the mid-19th century new centres of population acquired new Anglican churches. One of the grandest was All Saints' church, Oakleigh Road, funded by John Miles, which was consecrated in 1882. Its adjacent school followed shortly. This postcard was taken *c.*1920.

107 & 108. As the population expanded so did the number and range of Nonconformist chapels, many of which changed premises as their congregations grew. A rare survival typical of many first-stage buildings is the iron chapel built by the Primitive Methodists on East End Road in 1872; they moved on in 1905, leaving it to smaller sects. Also in East Finchley, the Catholics took over the former Congregational chapel in 1898. This building was destroyed in 1940 and its replacement is further north. The chapel had given its name to the adjacent Chapel Street, which linked Market Place and High Road until the 1960s' redevelopment. The Market Place end is now within Chapel Court.

109.   The approach to Whetstone, *c.*1880. York Villa, on the corner of Green Road, is today one of Whetstone's few surviving villas of the mid-19th century. Whetstone Place, the terrace on the left, came to a spectacular end in 1939 when it was burnt during an Air Raid Precautions emergency services' exercise.

110.   The junction of the High Road and Friern Barnet Lane in *c.*1890, showing the *Three Horseshoes* with the row of small cottages to its left and parade of similarly modest shops, known as Whetstone Parade, to its right.

111. Harper's bakery on the corner of Totteridge Lane had been established almost 50 years when this photograph was taken *c.*1890. The Harper family continued to run the shop until 1939 when it was taken over by a local rival, and renamed Hillside Bakeries the next year. Whetstone High Road did not become a 'modern' shopping area around the turn of the century, but inter- and post-war change has been so drastic that the bakery is now a rare survival.

112. A local carrier outside Bell Cottages at the northern end of Whetstone, *c.*1905. Beyond are Jaques Cottages and the *Blue Anchor*. All were replaced in the 1970s.

113. This picture of the Catchpole family was taken outside their home, again Bell Cottages, in 1896. The same plaque to J. Taylor, brickmaker, is visible above the door.

114. The Sailor's Home Refreshment Rooms next to the *Black Bull* in Whetstone was both a tea-room and a village store. It was run by Mrs. Beaumont (seen here in about 1920) and her ex-sailor husband.

115. This postcard of the eastern end of Woodhouse Lane (now Woodhouse Road) was sent in 1908 before suburban development began to encroach on the haystacks.

116. Goldsmith Road, pictured c.1915, was one of several roads developed on the Southgate Park estate in the 1890s. Similar houses on the adjoining Holly Park estate were dismissively described in 1904 as mainly the residences of London clerks keeping up appearances on small incomes.

117. The Parade, Friern Barnet Road, pictured in 1906. The Parade, which is opposite Friern Hospital, was originally built in the 1890s but extended in the 1900s over the grounds of the defunct Friern Barnet High School for Girls to the corner with Carlton Avenue shown here.

118. Friern Barnet Road at the junction with Station Road in *c.*1904, shortly after the building of Bank Parade on the right. The turretted building opposite is the much older *Railway Hotel* which dates back to the 1850s, although the turrets which gave the pub its later name had been added in an extension of 1887.

119. After decades of complaints, Friern Barnet was finally forced to develop a proper sewerage system, with a sewage farm which opened in 1883. This picture, commemorating a pipe being laid, also provides a detailed, and almost unrecognisable, view of the High Road at Whetstone.

120. Finchley attempted a cheap and inadequate solution to its sewage problems in 1867, but was finally compelled to build a proper system, with a sewage farm at Summers Lane, in 1885. The exact location within Finchley of this vivid photograph of pipe-laying is unknown.

121. Finchley U.D.C. formed a professional fire brigade in 1899, taking over the volunteer brigade premises established at a shop in Hendon Lane in 1888 and later extended into the adjoining shops. This photograph shows the brigade in the 1930s shortly before the station was replaced by a new one at the junction of the North Circular and Long Lane.

122. The Friern Avenue Laundry stood in three acres of ground at North Finchley. In this *c*.1905 advertisement the proprietress proudly announced that no chemicals were used and cordially invited inspection of the establishment. By 1928, however, the laundry, along with 13 others, had been swallowed up by Advance Cleaners and Launderers (London).

123. Finchley's splendid skating rink opened immediately south of the *Swan and Pyramids* in 1910, but very soon became the Rink cinema. This too was unsuccessful and from 1923 the building was the headquarters of Carrimore Six-Wheelers Ltd. It was demolished for the Metropolitan Police garage in 1970.

124. Plans for what is now the Phoenix cinema were approved in 1910, making it just possibly the oldest cinema in the country still in use. Since it opened in 1912 its exterior and interior, as well as its name, have all been altered several times.

"Bohemia"
FINCHLEY

BOHEMIA
WINTER GARDENS CINEMA

THE EXTERIOR

WINTER AND SUMMER GARDENS
CINEMA .. VAUDEVILLE .. THEATRE
BALL ROOM . . . CONCERT HALL
RESTAURANT . . . BANQUET HALL
(To be ready in Spring)
. . . . . YE OLDE WORLD TEA ANNEXE . . . . .

Open from 2.30 to 10.30 :: :: On Saturday to 11 p.m.

The One Admission Fee of Sixpence covers all the Entertainments

Programme - - ONE PENNY

125.   The Bohemia in Ballards Lane was obviously flourishing when this programme was produced in 1915. But success was short-lived and it was replaced in 1920 by the more modest, and modern, New Bohemia cinema. The original Bohemia was between Princes and Redbourne Avenues. The New Bohemia, which survived until 1959, was further south on the site now occupied by Gateway House.

126.   The *Railway Hotel* on the junction of Ballards Lane and Nether Street seen in about 1909. Like many of its rivals it was offering a wide range of facilities, including 'a handsome billiard room with adjoining coffee room, well-equipped in every respect ...'. It was demolished in 1962 and replaced by a characterless office block and a new pub called *The Minstrel*.

127.   The East Finchley Cricket Club in the 1893 season. The club was founded in 1880 and had grounds on East End Road where Ossulton Way is now. It had disbanded by 1911, and members probably joined the Finchley Cricket Club, which existed by the 1830s and had recently acquired new grounds further north on East End Road.

128. East End Road at the turn of the century, with the old East Finchley Cricket Club ground on the right. Ossulton Way was cut through this in about 1930. Park Farm, the home of 'Lord' George Sanger, is in the background.

WILD ANIMALS UNDER THE HAMMER: THE SALE AT FINCHLEY OF THE STOCK OF LORD GEORGE SANGER, LIMITED.

A CIRCUS AT AUCTION.

In consequence of legal complications, Messrs. J. Odell and Co. were instructed to sell by auction yesterday (and the sale will continue to-day) the "live and dead stock and plant, 200 horses, ponies, and mules, four trained elephants, four camels, lions, tigers, leopards, hyenas, and monkeys; parade carriages, beast wagons, and chariots, and 500 costumes, forming the circus of Lord George (the original) Sanger, Limited." The sale began at Mr. Sanger's farm at Finchley yesterday, but only the horses, ponies, and mules came under the hammer. The wild beasts are to be sold to-day.

The auctioneer's stand was a show wagon, and the sale took place in a long shed, within which is a training ring. In a corner, placidly awaiting their fate on the morrow, were the elephants and camels. Into the ring came the equine "lots," one after another, and the best of them were, it is said, bought by Mr. Sanger himself. Rome was not built in a day, a performing horse is not taught in an hour, and an old showman knows what he is about.

129. For a number of years while 'Lord' George Sanger leased Park Farm the procession of his animals to winter quarters there was a favourite local spectacle. Even more famous than the 1903 auction, recorded here by the *Daily Graphic*, was Sanger's murder there by one of his servants in 1911.

130. Nether Court was in Hendon when it was built, on a lavish scale, by Henry Tubbs in 1883. In 1892 he allowed the Finchley Golf Club to open in part of the grounds, but the club lapsed in the First World War. It was refounded in 1930 taking the whole estate, which in 1933 was transferred into Finchley.

131. The East Finchley Board School in Long Lane opened in 1884, after three years of using temporary Congregational premises in Chapel Street. Later known as the Alder School, it was merged with Christ's College in 1978 and the buildings demolished. This carefully segregated school photograph was taken c.1912.

132 & 133.   Both these Catholic convent schools began as fee-paying schools but later became maintained. St Michael's, the earliest Catholic school in Finchley, opened in 1908. Marie Auxiliatrice occupied Finchley Manor House from 1921 until its merger into Bishop Douglass in 1969. The postcards show the St Michael's dining room and Marie Auxiliatrice's laboratory.

134.   There was a plethora of private schools established throughout the area from the 1880s to the 1910s, usually in large houses like Cambridge House or Clevedon featured in this Finchley U.D.C. brochure of 1910. Like the U.D.C., the builders of new middle-class estates were fond of advertising them in their brochures, but most were small and short-lived. Few survived after the Second World War.

Etchingham Park School (Girls), Church End, Finchley, N.   Preparation for the Oxford Local Examinations and the School Examinations of the Associated Board of the Royal Academy of Music and the Royal College of Music, &c.

Etchingham Park School (Boys), Church End, Finchley, N.   Thorough preparation for the Public Schools.   Principals : The Misses Coatsworth.

At *Cambridge House*, Nether Street, Miss Nathan undertakes the education of the daughters of gentlemen.   She prepares in the ordinary school course for London Matriculation and the various other English and Music Examinations. There are Kindergarten and Transition Classes to which boys under nine are admitted.   Cambridge House is beautifully situated, overlooking the open country to the North.

Finchley High School for Boys.   " Clevedon," 12, Thyra Grove, North Finchley. Established 1892.   Principal : Mr. Samuel B. Vernon, for ten years assistant master at Southgate Road Middle Class School; two years at Rothbury House College, twelve years head master of Victoria College, Stroud Green.   This school affords to boys belonging to the Middle Classes a sound practical and liberal education, and is adapted to prepare them for commercial, professional or scientific pursuits, although it is mainly commercial.   Fees, Boarders from 25 guineas per annum ; Day Pupils from 4 to 6 guineas per annum.   Prospectus sent on application to the Principal.

Physical culture is much to the fore in Finchley, and is in the hands of highly experienced teachers.   The Misses Wilson hold classes for physical culture and gymnastics at the following centres :—Highgate, Muswell Hill, High Barnet, and North Finchley.   Classes are also held in connection with Holmewood School in the Woodside Hall.   Private instruction and treatment are given in Swedish Medical Gymnastics, Massage and Electricity.   For further particulars apply to the Misses Wilson, St. Cuthbert's, Friern Park, North Finchley.

36

Finchley Cottage Hospital.

A PUBLIC MEETING

Will be held at the District Council Offices, Church End,

On THURSDAY, 29th JUNE, 1905, at 8 p.m.

SIR ALFRED DE BOCK PORTER, K.C.B.,

IN THE CHAIR.

"Strenuous efforts have been made to raise the requisite funds.   In October last a circular letter, appealing for money to erect the building, was sent to every householder in the district, about 6,000 in number, and a personal canvass from house to house has since been made over the greater part of the district.   The Committee regret to say that, with few exceptions, the response, so far, has not been equal to their reasonable expectations.   Grateful mention must, however, be made of subscriptions received from the working-men, who have already collected amongst themselves a sum of £169 8s. 5d., and are still making regular weekly contributions.

135 & 136.   Finchley's need for a cottage hospital was widely agreed, but raising enough funds proved difficult, as this extract from a 1905 meeting makes plain. The hospital finally opened in 1908. After 1918 a new appeal funded its enlargement, and in 1922 the War Memorial Extension was opened and the hospital's name changed from Cottage to Memorial Hospital.

137 & 138.   The Finchley Carnival was born as a fund-raising scheme for the hospital, and its proceeds continued to maintain the two carnival beds. Both these pictures were taken before the hospital opened.

139. Victoria Park opened in 1902 in commemoration of the Queen's Diamond Jubilee, an earlier attempt to mark her Golden Jubilee having failed. It remained Finchley's only public park until 1914. Those enjoying it here include a lady in a wheelchair and a baby in a pram.

140. Friary Park was opened in May 1910, although the official ceremony was cancelled because of the death of Edward VII, to whom as 'the peacemaker' its statue of Peace was dedicated. The park was immediately popular even though the surrounding area was not yet fully developed.

141.   Avenue House was built in 1859 but greatly altered by Henry C. Stephens after he bought it in 1874. 'Inky' Stephens (his father invented the famous ink) had his laboratory there. He was also M.P. for Hornsey (which included Finchley and Friern) from 1887-1900 and acted locally as 'the uncrowned king of Finchley'. On his death in 1918 he bequeathed his house and beautifully landscaped grounds to the people of Finchley. The house was Finchley's Council Offices from 1940. It was severely damaged by fire in 1989.

142. The Woodside Hall was built by the proprietor of Woodside estate, Henry Holden, in 1885. It survived this sale and continued as a public hall until becoming the North Finchley and Woodside Park district synagogue in 1950.

143. The Stephens Memorial Hall at Tally Ho commemorated the vicar of Christ Church who had died in 1898 rather than his better known namesake at Avenue House. The hall, which was used for a wide range of activities, was sold in 1938 and a new one built behind the church. The site is now part of Owen Owen.

144 & 145. King Edward Hall was built at the junction of Regents Park Road and Hendon Lane in 1911 and provided accommodation for social functions. During the First World War, like many buildings, it became a temporary hospital.

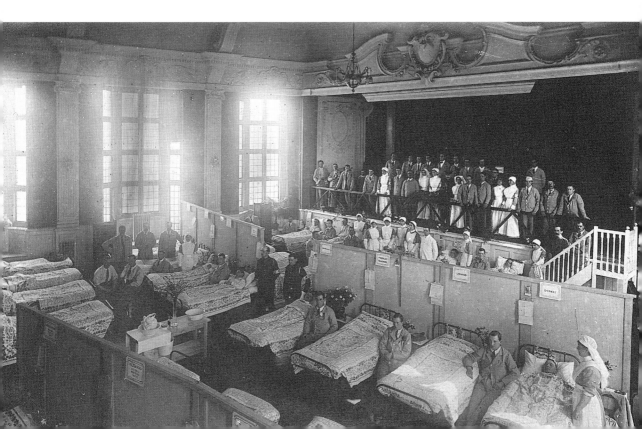

146.   Many women volunteered as auxiliary nurses, and the sewing seen here would have been one of their rare lighter duties.

147. Finchley residents in 1913 and 1914 vigorously fought and defeated two Northern Junction Railway schemes for a line connecting Ealing and Brentford to the G.N.R. mainline at Wood Green. Their fears of spoiled land values and amenities are well illustrated in this poster. After the war most of the fields in any case vanished, and the lines of both rail schemes were used by new arterial roads: the Great North Way and the North Circular.

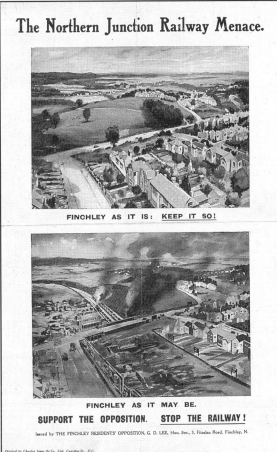

The Northern Junction Railway Menace.

FINCHLEY AS IT IS: KEEP IT SO!

FINCHLEY AS IT MAY BE.
SUPPORT THE OPPOSITION.   STOP THE RAILWAY!

Issued by THE FINCHLEY RESIDENTS' OPPOSITION, G. D. LEE, Hon. Sec., 3, Fitzalan Road, Finchley, N.

Printed by Charles Jones & Co. Ltd. Cursitor St., E.C.

148. The children of Market Place gathered at the Jackson family's coal wharf in Chapel Street in about 1917.

149 & 150.   The earlier picture shows the range of carriers who used *The Cricketers* at Tally Ho (currently the *Coach Stop*) in 1900. By 1920, when the second picture was taken, the scene was much quieter. This was a temporary lull before the 1935 Kingsway redevelopment incorporated this top section of Nether Street.

151. New houses on the Friern Watch estate advertised in a 1920s' brochure. The original house was retained within three acres until the 1970s as the St Elizabeth's Home for Incurable Women, later St Elizabeth's Hospital, but the remaining 42 acres were sold by the original development company, Newcombe Estates, as small plots to builders, often local, who had to build to the company's specifications.

152. Although the former estate of the Duke of Buckingham and Chandos was sold in 1892, only Chandos Avenue was put through before 1914, and even there only the eastern end was developed. Building was not completed until the 1920s, when this picture was taken, and when the other roads also appeared.

153. High Road Whetstone as it looked *c.*1923. The old *Swan with Two Necks* seen on the left was demolished in 1960. The billboard beyond is advertising new houses on the Birley Road estate for sale at £795.

154. Lawson's timber merchants was established in 1921 and still runs from this site on Whetstone High Road. There has been some rebuilding and extension, though, and the landmark chimney (which ventilated the sewer gases) has disappeared.

155. Watercress growing was another local industry. These beds on the Mutton Brook near the site of Henley's Corner lasted well into the 20th century.

156. The North Circular and Falloden Way, the latter leading to the new A1, were both built in the 1920s. This view, taken in 1933, looks eastward across the Finchley Road to their junction. The garage which bequeathed its name to Henley's Corner was not yet built.

157.   Just to the north, the moment of Lloyd George's unveiling of *La Delivrance* in 1927. The statue was sculpted by Guillaume and inspired by the Allied victory at the Battle of the Marne. It was bought by Viscount Rothermere who presented it to Finchley in memory of his mother.

158. This was the *Manor Cottage Tavern* at the junction of East End Road and Green Lane in about 1912. After the coming of the North Circular, just to the left, in the 1920s the tavern was rebuilt and Green Lane became redundant. It no longer bridges the railway but its ends both here and at Long Lane can still be discovered.

159. Outings organised by local groups were a regular feature of summer life, particularly after the coming of motor transport. This East Finchley group travelled to Brighton in 1924 in a car which had been built by its driver.

160. The tollhouse at *Spaniards*, lying just within Finchley, marks the point where Hampstead Lane left the Bishop of London's park. The inn has been a favourite for excursions since at least the 18th century, and was the place where the mob was halted while on its way to attack Kenwood during the Gordon Riots in 1780. This photograph shows cars negotiating the bottleneck in 1935.

161. On the forecourt of *The Griffin* inn at Whetstone, this bus is on route 551 to Edmonton in 1927.

162.   Tally Ho became one of the main centres of the Metropolitan Tramway Company. The picture shows trams at the newly-created terminus at Kingsway which opened in 1935, three years before the trams were superceded by trolleybuses.

163. This cottage, curiously known as The Frenchman's Gussett, lay on Frenchmans Farm on the eastern side of Friern Barnet Lane above Holly Park. The farm was offered for development in the 1870s but continued to produce more hay than houses until the 1920s.

164. Brook Farm on the western side of Whetstone High Road shortly before its demolition in 1914. Its lands had been acquired by Finchley U.D.C. in 1912 to provide cricket and football pitches and allotments.

165. While fields remained, the growing suburban demand for milk ensured that local dairy farms flourished. Among these was Oakleigh Park Farm, also known as Manor Farm, whose frontage on the High Road at Whetstone was immediately south of where Chandos Avenue is now.

166. An advertisement *c*.1900 for Jersey Farm dairies, which had also acquired Court House Farm on Nether Street and had cow sheds at Ballards Lane and Friern Park.

THE JERSEY FARM DAIRIES.

MILK THAT IS "FRESH" FROM THE COW

versus

"REFRIGERATED" OR RAILWAY MILK.

HERE is no article of Diet which is of such importance as "Fresh" MILK, and to sustain the health of children and those who drink it as a beverage, it is absolutely necessary it should be "Fresh from the Cow."

It certainly behoves Families to be more particular as to the source of their Milk supply to ensure its being wholesome. It would be most beneficial to the public if the Food Adulteration Act insisted that all Milk sold should be "Fresh," this, naturally, being most essential in an article so susceptible to putrefactive changes, and now that so much "stale" Milk comes from the Country, and from places under no **supervision** whatever, and where it is passed over a metallic "Refrigerator," which destroys the natural delicate quality, and materially reduces its nutritious elements.

In this state it reaches the "Middleman" or Milk seller—too often entirely **ignorant** of the production and properties of Milk, who serves it to his customers as a **pure article,** but without the great "desideratum" of its being "Fresh."

167. Floats of the Farm Dairies Ltd. in Church Lane, East Finchley, on parade for Finchley Carnival *c.*1935-6. This block of buildings was demolished *c.*1963 and replaced with flats.

168 & 169. College Farm, earlier Sheephouse Farm, was acquired in 1868 by George Barham of Express Dairies, who rebuilt it as a Model Dairy Farm. Uniquely among the farms of Finchley and Friern it still survives, although now featuring rare breeds rather than dairy herds and stack yards.

170. Argyle Road started as the Finchley end of a footpath which crossed the Dollis Brook at Frith Bridge. This 1900 view shows the track continuing westward towards Jersey Farm. The road was named in the 1890s but houses were not developed until the 1920s.

171. Finchley's last shepherdess, Mrs. Lily Mortimer, pictured in 1934. Her sheep were grazed over the fields between East End Road and Hampstead Heath until restricted by the inter-war development of the Finchley side of Hampstead Garden Suburb.

172. Finchley U.D.C. bought part of the Woodhouse estate for housing in 1915, building some houses immediately and a second wave from 1919. The picture shows Ingleway nearing completion in June 1921.

173. Red Lion Hill looking north in 1938. The left-hand third of the view remains today but the rest was soon to be replaced by the Red Lion Hill Housing Scheme – now the Grange estate. The area's historic name of Cuckolds Haven had already lapsed.

174 & 175. The Red Lion Hill or Grange estate under construction in 1938. It included what is now the Oak Lane Health Centre, shown here when it opened.

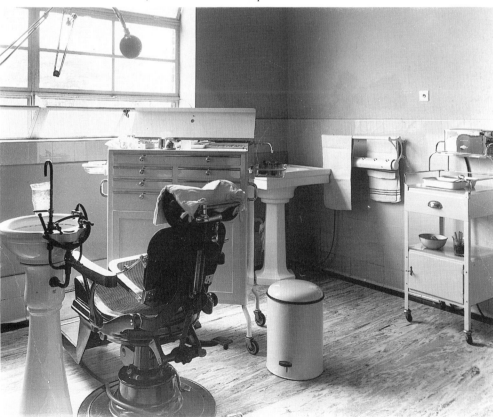

176. Windermere Avenue seen from the corner of Beechwood Avenue in January 1932. The prominent 'For Sale' sign names King and Freeman of Golders Green as the builders and owners.

ETCHINGHAM COUR

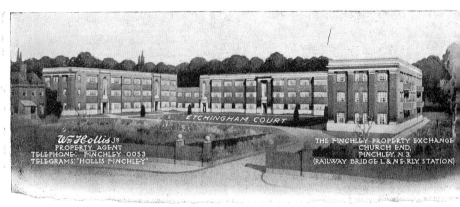

Wm Hollis JR
PROPERTY AGENT
TELEPHONE: FINCHLEY 0053
TELEGRAMS: "HOLLIS FINCHLEY"

THE FINCHLEY PROPERTY EXCHANGE
CHURCH END,
FINCHLEY, N.3.
(RAILWAY BRIDGE L.& N.E. RLY. STATION)

Three Types of Flats—

    Two bedrooms one reception, to three bedrooms one reception room, or two bedrooms, two reception rooms. kitchen and bathroom.

The rooms have large windows, a special feature being bay windows to the lounge.

Rents from £100 per annum inclusive rates, taxes and constant hot wa

Garages available at £15 per annum.

Uniformed porter in attendance.

Furnished flat can now be viewed.

Particulars from Letting Office at Etchingham Court or WILLIAM HOLLIS JNR., The

INCHLEY N 3

CHINGHAM COURT is situated in ETCHINGHAM PARK
ROAD, near Granville Road, one of the best roads in Church End,
ey. The position is unique, for it provides well appointed Flats very
to London, but with a completely rural view from any window.

lesign and detail of the building are the work of Mr. Austin Blomfield,
, A.R.I.B.A., of New Court, E.C.4—who has received his training and
ience under Sir Reginald Blomfield, M.A., R.A., one of the leading
tects of Great Britain—in collaboration with Mr. B. Ewart Dixon, the
nown local Architect, and as a result of their very wide experience,
gnified design, planning and domestic architectural detail could not be
ved upon in order that occupiers may run their flats with a minimum
nt of labour and expense.

roup of Flats stands in the middle of a garden which is surrounded by a matured
trees.

ardens will be maintained by the Landlords and will give the residents the
of sheltered and delightful surroundings.

Flat is provided with a coal fireplace in one room and gas fires in the bedrooms,
l the Flats are supplied with a constant supply of hot water which tends to keep
ole building at a regular temperature.

itchen is fitted with useful modern conveniences and each Flat is provided with coal
ist bins placed immediately behind the back door on a porch specially built for the
se.

is room for Tennis Courts in the grounds which will be kept for the private use
joyment of the residents.

s to the Flats is gained by a private drive bordered by flower beds and encircling
tire building, thus enabling the tenants to drive direct to their own particular
ce.

y Exchange, Church End, Finchley. Phone Fin. 0053

177. *(left)* Etchingham Court, dating from 1935, is typical of the many speculatively-built blocks of service flats which were beginning to appear in the area. At over £100 a year their attraction lay not in economy but in their often advertised labour-saving qualities and their epitome of modern living.

178. *(below left)* Finchley's first swimming baths opened in Squires Lane in 1915. Shown here is the open-air pool which was opened in 1931 and became more famous, embodying as it does both the architecture and the spirit of the decade.

179. *(below)* Finchley ratepayers had pressed for public libraries for many years, but it was not until 1933 that one was opened in Avenue House. North Finchley Library, shown here at its opening, followed in 1936, and East Finchley in 1938. Friern shared the school premises-based county library service from 1925 and acquired its first purpose-built library in 1934.

Here is the Gaumont Finchley

a modern cinema in every detail, equipped for efficient service, with comfortable, pleasant and healthy surroundings in which to enjoy your entertainment.

The Decoration and Lighting has been carried out in the modern Swedish style, yet nevertheless it is unobtrusive and gives a perfect air of restfulness, which is so important in a place of entertainment.

The materials used in construction, the luxurious furnishings and fittings are all of British manufacture, and the theatre stands as a monument to the efficiency of British workmanship.

Architect : W. E. TRENT, Esq., F.R.I.B.A., F.S.I.
Assistant Architects : W. Sydney Trent, Esq., F.R.I.B.A.
R. Golding, Esq.
Electrical Engineer : S. HART, Esq., M.I.E.E.
Builders : Messrs. McLAUGHLIN & HARVEY, LTD.

180.   The Gaumont at Tally Ho was the last word in cinema design at its grand opening, performed by the Mayor of Finchley in 1937, and it became an important local focus. It was demolished in 1987.

181. This photograph from 1940 shows both the old and new Friern U.D.C. headquarters. In the foreground is The Priory, the 18th-century house which had served as the U.D.C. offices since 1906 and was demolished in 1941 when the new town hall, designed in quintessential period style, was completed.

182. The 393 (Finchley) Squadron Air Training Corps soon after its formation in 1941. This together with the 1825 (East Finchley) Squadron formed the Finchley Wing A.T.C. under the command of Squadron Leader J. M. Henderson, shown here taking the salute at Avenue House.

183. Avenue House grounds were the setting for many public functions, concerts and plays in the 1930s, and were host to the Victory celebrations of 9 May 1945.